Yean Li Ho

Heuristic Cryptanalysis of Classical and Modern Ciphers

Yean Li Ho

Heuristic Cryptanalysis of Classical and Modern Ciphers

LAP LAMBERT Academic Publishing

Impressum / Imprint
Bibliografische Information der Deutschen Nationalbibliothek: Die Deutsche Nationalbibliothek verzeichnet diese Publikation in der Deutschen Nationalbibliografie; detaillierte bibliografische Daten sind im Internet über http://dnb.d-nb.de abrufbar. Alle in diesem Buch genannten Marken und Produktnamen unterliegen warenzeichen-, marken- oder patentrechtlichem Schutz bzw. sind Warenzeichen oder eingetragene Warenzeichen der jeweiligen Inhaber. Die Wiedergabe von Marken, Produktnamen, Gebrauchsnamen, Handelsnamen, Warenbezeichnungen u.s.w. in diesem Werk berechtigt auch ohne besondere Kennzeichnung nicht zu der Annahme, dass solche Namen im Sinne der Warenzeichen- und Markenschutzgesetzgebung als frei zu betrachten wären und daher von jedermann benutzt werden dürften.

Bibliographic information published by the Deutsche Nationalbibliothek: The Deutsche Nationalbibliothek lists this publication in the Deutsche Nationalbibliografie; detailed bibliographic data are available in the Internet at http://dnb.d-nb.de.
Any brand names and product names mentioned in this book are subject to trademark, brand or patent protection and are trademarks or registered trademarks of their respective holders. The use of brand names, product names, common names, trade names, product descriptions etc. even without a particular marking in this work is in no way to be construed to mean that such names may be regarded as unrestricted in respect of trademark and brand protection legislation and could thus be used by anyone.

Coverbild / Cover image: www.ingimage.com

Verlag / Publisher:
LAP LAMBERT Academic Publishing
ist ein Imprint der / is a trademark of
OmniScriptum GmbH & Co. KG
Heinrich-Böcking-Str. 6-8, 66121 Saarbrücken, Deutschland / Germany
Email: info@lap-publishing.com

Herstellung: siehe letzte Seite /
Printed at: see last page
ISBN: 978-3-659-69140-9

I dedicate this book to Fr. M, Fr. Fab and my brother, Eric.
You are the reason this was possible.

I would also like to remember my parents and my sister.

TABLE OF CONTENTS

4

Abstract

Block cipher algorithms are commonly used to secure confidential information in everyday user applications like smart cards. However, it is quite common for ignorant users to use familiar dictionary words or even names as their personal passwords. This book aims to examine the effects of weakly chosen *password-keys* on the security of *block ciphers*. Two *optimisation heuristic cryptanalytic attack methods* (*Tabu Search* and *Genetic Algorithm*) are used to conduct *intelligent key-search attacks* on *classical ciphers* and *modern ciphers*. These attacks *are* based on *linguistic frequencies* identified in the English Language. The *classical ciphers* examined are the *Hill Cipher* (a *substitution cipher*) and the *Columnar Transposition Cipher* (a *permutation / transposition cipher*). The algorithm chosen to represent *modern block ciphers* is the Advanced Encryption Standard (AES) algorithm (also known as *"Rijndael"*). AES is an algebraic *product cipher* which combines elements of *substitution* (*ByteSub, MixColumns* and *AddRoundKey* step) and *transposition ciphers* (*ShiftRows* step). As there has yet to be a study on *optimisation heuristic attacks* against *product ciphers*, this book aims to study the effects of an *optimisation heuristic cryptanalytic attack* on a *modern block cipher*. The results show that the *Tabu Search* attacks works well against all three *ciphers*. However, the *Genetic Algorithm* attacks work best against the *transposition cipher* (*Columnar Transposition Cipher*). The *Product Cipher* (*AES*) is the most secure and stable against the *optimisation heuristic attacks;* followed by the *Polygraphic Substitution Cipher* (*Hill Cipher*) and the *Transposition Cipher* (*Columnar Transposition Cipher*). Regardless of the *strength* and *security* of the *cipher algorithm,* weak passwords are vulnerable to attacks by the average *hacker* or *script kiddie* using a basic personal computer system.

Chapter 1 – Introduction

In today's *K-Economy* where knowledge means power, *cryptology*[1] is an integral part of the study of securing information and preventing confidential data from falling into the wrong hands. *"Cryptanalysis is the branch of cryptology dealing with the breaking of a cipher* [2] *to recover information, or forging encrypted information that will be accepted as authentic"* (Stallings, 2003).

There are 2 main types of *cryptographic* algorithms: *symmetric-key* and *asymmetric* (*public-key*) algorithms. *Symmetric-key* algorithms can be divided into 2 categories: *block ciphers* and *stream ciphers*. Figure 1 illustrates the different classifications of *Cryptographic ciphers*.

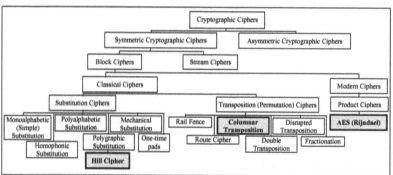

Figure 1: Schematic representation of cryptographic cipher classification (adapted from Gründlingh and Van Vuuren; [Schneier,1996] and Search Spaniel.com).

This research project attempts to extend the works of (Clark and Dawson, 1998) and (Dimovski and Gligoroski, October 2003). This study is aimed at examining the application of an *optimisation heuristic cryptanalytic* attack on weakly chosen *keys* in *block ciphers*; namely *classical ciphers* and *modern ciphers*. A *block cipher* is a

---

[1] *"Crypto algorithms are the equivalent of locks, seals, security stamps and identification documents on the Internet. They are essential to protect our on-line bank transactions, credit cards, and personal information and to support e-commerce and e-government"* (NESSIE, Project, 2003).

[2] *"Breaking a cipher simply means finding a weakness in the cipher that can be exploited with a complexity less than brute-force"* (Schneier, 1998).

7

symmetric-key cryptographic cipher which uses the same *secret key* to *encrypt* [3] as well as *decrypt* fixed blocks of a *secret* message. There are two categories of *classical ciphers*: *substitution ciphers* and *transposition (permutation) ciphers*. Most *modern ciphers* are *product ciphers*, which are extensions of *classical ciphers*. A *product cipher* is a *block cipher* which is an amalgam of components made of *substitution* and *transposition* ciphers (Gründlingh and Van Vuuren).

Hence, experiments will be conducted to examine and compare the effectiveness of using *tabu search* or *genetic algorithm* based on *character frequency statistics* to recover *messages encrypted* by weakly chosen *keys* in *block ciphers*. (Clark and Dawson, 1998) conducted their research on the least secure *substitution cipher*, namely the *simple substitution cipher*. Here, a more secure *substitution cipher* will be considered: the *polygraphic substitution cipher*. (Dimovski and Gligoroski, October 2003) also conducted their research on the most basic *transposition cipher*, whereas a more complex *permutation algorithm* will be studied here. To date, an attack of such a nature has yet to be tested out on a *product cipher* but its behaviour will be observed here. This work will be further extended to compare the security of the three major categories of *cipher algorithms (substitution ciphers, transposition ciphers* and *product ciphers)* against such an attack.

The Advanced Encryption Standard (AES) has been chosen to represent the group of *modern ciphers* because it is a relatively new *product cipher*. Among all the *transposition ciphers*, the *Columnar Transposition Cipher* which is most similar to the *ShiftRows* step of the AES *algorithm* will be studied as well. Since the *Hill Cipher* is also quite similar to the *SubBytes* step of the *AES algorithm*, the *Hill Cipher* is chosen to represent the *substitution ciphers* in this study.

Chapter 2 provides the reader with some background knowledge of this domain. It briefly describes the different *block ciphers (substitution, transposition* and *product ciphers)*; highlighting the chosen sample for each type. As *heuristic cryptanalytic attacks* have yet to be applied on *product ciphers*, Chapter 2 briefly outlines the existing *cryptanalytic* efforts conducted on AES (the chosen example of a *product cipher*) and related *heuristic* attacks on *classical ciphers*. It also introduces *linguistic frequencies* as a *heuristic function* following a brief introduction to the *tabu search* algorithm and the *genetic algorithm*. Chapter 3 describes the methodology to be tested on samples of all three types of *block ciphers* while Chapter 4 summarizes and

---

[3] *"Encryption algorithms are essential to protect sensitive information such as medical data, financial information and Personal Identification Numbers (PINs) from prying eyes"* (NESSIE Project, 2003).

discusses the results of the study conducted. Finally, Chapter 5 takes a look at the ramifications of this research and how this study can be further extended.

Chapter 2 – Related Work

2.1 The Substitution Cipher (The *Polygraphic Hill Cipher*)

A *substitution cipher* maintains the original position of a *plaintext* character in the *ciphertext* but substitutes the value of a *plaintext* character or character string with another value (Gründlingh and Van Vuuren). A *Polygraphic Cipher* substitutes blocks of characters in groups; usually pairs of characters known as *bigrams* (Search Spaniel.com).

The *Hill cipher* was invented by Lester S. Hill in 1929 (Stallings, 2003). It is a *polygraphic substitution* algorithm which combines and substitutes groups of letters in a block matrix using *linear* algebra. There are a total of 26 alphabets and each letter is treated as a digit in base 26: A = 0, B =1, etc.

Suppose that there are n distinct plaintext-ciphertext pairs where:
X= (n x n) matrix of plaintext characters at location i,
Y= (n x n) matrix of ciphertext characters at the corresponding location i, and
K = (n x n) matrix of the Key
Therefore, Y=XK mod 26 and K=X^{-1}Y mod 26 (Stallings, 2003).

To ensure that decryption is possible, *"the components of the matrix are the key, and should be random provided that the matrix is invertible in GF (26^n)... A block of n letters is then considered as a vector of n dimensions, and multiplied by a (n x n) matrix, modulo 26"* (SearchSpaniel.com). An example quoted by (Stallings, 2003) is described in Figure 2 (below).

Suppose Plaintext	: Friday (Numerical conversion: 5 17 8 3 0 24)
Ciphertext	: PQCFKU (Numerical conversion: 15 16 2 5 10 19)

And n=2(*bigram*),　　e_k(f,r)=(P,Q),　　e_k(i,d)=(C,F),　　e_k(a,y)=(K,U)

Then,　　$\begin{pmatrix} 15 & 16 \\ 2 & 5 \end{pmatrix} = \begin{pmatrix} 5 & 17 \\ 8 & 3 \end{pmatrix} K$

Therefore,　　$K = \begin{pmatrix} 5 & 17 \\ 8 & 3 \end{pmatrix}^{-1} \begin{pmatrix} 15 & 16 \\ 2 & 5 \end{pmatrix} = \begin{pmatrix} 9 & 1 \\ 2 & 15 \end{pmatrix} \begin{pmatrix} 15 & 16 \\ 2 & 5 \end{pmatrix} = \begin{pmatrix} 7 & 19 \\ 8 & 3 \end{pmatrix}$

Figure 2: An example showing the *Hill Cipher encryption* process (Stallings, 2003)

According to Stallings (2003), the frequency distribution of bigrams is more evenly spread in *Polygraphic ciphers* like the *Hill Cipher* as compared to the frequency distribution of individual letters in a *Monoalphabetic cipher*. This makes it more difficult to break the *ciphertext*. It is difficult to break the *Hill Cipher* based on *known-ciphertext* only. However the *linearity* of the *Hill Cipher* makes it vulnerable to *known-plaintext* attacks. Hence, the *cipher* is usually combined with a *permutation* or *transposition* component in *Modern Ciphers* like *Feistel Ciphers* (Search Spaniel.com).

2.2   The Transposition Cipher (The *Columnar Transposition Cipher*)

The *transposition cipher* rearranges the positions of the *plaintext* characters in a different and usually complex order but *"leaves the value of a character or character string unaltered when transforming plaintext into Ciphertext"* (Gründlingh and Van Vuuren). The *Columnar TranspositionCipher* arranges the *plaintext* in a square matrix from left to right and from top to bottom. It depends on the *key* to determine the number of columns for the letters in the square. Each *character* in the *key* becomes a column *header* followed by the *plaintext message* in successive rows beneath those *headers*. Spaces are ignored or replaced with a *"null"* value. Finally, the *encrypted* message is written in groups according to columns (in alphabetical order of the *headers*) (SearchSpaniel.com).

Suppose Plaintext	: WE HAVE TO UNDERSTAND HOW THIS WORKS
Key	: SECRET.

To encrypt the text, write the key on the first line and number the letters of the keyword in alphabetical order. (Duplicate letters (like the "E") are numbered from left to right.

Order Read	5 2 1 4 3 6
Key(Column Size)	S E C R E T
Plaintext	W E H A V E
	T O U N D E
	R S T A N D
	H O W T H I
	S W O R K S

The resulting *ciphertext*: HUTWO EOSOW VDNHK ANATR WTRHS EEDIS

10

Figure 3: An example showing the *Columnar Transposition Cipher encryption process*

As shown above, the transposition cipher basically rearranges the content according to a regular pattern. This could be made more complex by additional shuffling the positions of the characters. However, the permutation component in a *modern cipher* like the AES algorithm (*ShiftRows* step) may not necessarily depend on the *key*.

2.3   The Modern Cipher (The AES Algorithm [NIST, 2001])

Advanced Encryption Standard (AES) is the latest *symmetric-key modern cipher algorithm* introduced by the US National Institute of Standards and Technology (NIST) and the US Federal Information Processing Standards (FIPS). *'Rijndael'* was designed by Rijmen and Daemen and chosen out of 21 *algorithms* to be the official AES *algorithm* on October 2, 2000. It is a *symmetric-key block cipher* which *encrypts* fixed *blocks* of 128 *bits* for a minimum of 10 *rounds* with a 128 *bit key* (NIST, 2001)[4]. For a 128 *bit key*, a *brute-force exhaustive key search attack*[5] would require 2^{128} *encryptions* to correctly guess the *key* used to *encrypt* a secret message. This would take approximately 5.4×10^{18} years provided 1 million *encryptions* are done every microsecond (Stallings, 2003:29).

AES was designed to overcome the weaknesses and flaws discovered in the design of the Data Encryption Standard (DES). This improved algorithm was meant to be a replacement for DES or triple DES (which is currently the most widely used *modern cipher* in many hardware and software implementations like smart cards). In addition to that, the designers of *'Rijndael'* claim that the common means of *modern cipher cryptanalytic attacks* (such as *differential, truncated differential, linear and interpolation attacks)* are ineffective against AES due to its design structure (Daemen and Rijmen, 1999). Many important commercial and government systems which currently use triple DES (Schneier, 2000) may eventually move to AES for the

---

[4] The *AES* Standard allows the *key length* to be increased to 192 *bits* (12 *rounds*) or 256 *bits* (14 *rounds*) for increased *security* (NIST, 2001).

[5] For any *symmetric-key cipher*, the most obvious means of attack is through *exhaustive key search* (Danielyan, 2000), which is dependent on the *key length*. Only a select group (like major government organisations with big budgets) can afford to conduct experiments of such a nature. However, due to the requirements of time and the limitations of *processing power* (hardware technology - both current and future) available, it is highly impractical since the minimum *key length* for *Rijndael* is 128 bits (Stallings, 2003:29).

security of sensitive data[6]. *"However, compared to the analysis of DES, the amount of time and the number of cryptographers devoted to analysing Rijndael are quite limited"* (Stallings, 2003). Therefore, this paper will attempt to discover the effects of weak *keys* in one of the more secure and less studied of *Modern cipher* algorithms, namely *Rijndael*.

2.3.1 The AES Algorithm [NIST, 2001]

As shown in Figure 4 (below), the AES *encryption* algorithm basically receives two inputs: a secret 128-*bit symmetric cipher key*[7] and a 128-*bit* message *block* to be *encrypted* (*plaintext*). After 10 *rounds* of *encryption*, the final *output* would be a *block* of undecipherable *garbage*, known as the *cipher text* (the encoded message).

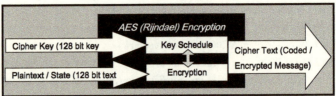

Figure 4: The Basic AES Encryption Algorithm

During the *encryption* process, the 128-*bit cipher key* will go through the *key schedule* process to produce 10 *sub-keys* for each *round* of the 10-*round encryption* algorithm. Figure 5 shows a summarised version of the *key schedule*. The diagram illustrates the steps needed to produce the 1st *round key*. The steps are repeated to produce subsequent *round keys* in a chain-like process with the previous calculated values (*RotWord*) as illustrated in Figure 5 (below).

The 128-*bit plaintext* block will go through the encryption process as shown above (Figure 6). Each round contains the 4 basic steps (the *ByteSub* step, the *ShiftRows* step, the *MixColumns* step and the *AddRoundKey* step), except for the final *round* (10th *round*) which omits the *MixColumns* step. In the initial round, the

---

[6] *See (NSA,2003; NESSIE Consortium,2003). "...the NESSIE project forms the bridge between the research community and the user community by testing and comparing algorithms before standardising them. The NESSIE project intends to input these algorithms to standardisation bodies such as ISO (International Organisation for Standardisation) and the IETF(Internet Engineering Task Force)" (NESSIE Project,2003).* For more information on NESSIE, see http://www.cryptonessie.org

[7] If the *key* is 192 *bits* or 256 *bits*, the number of *encryption rounds* would be 12 and 14 respectively. This explanation follows the default standard chosen, which uses 10 *rounds* of *encryption* and a 128-bit *key*. However, the same method also applies if the *key length* is increased to 192 *bits* or 256 *bits*. Correspondingly, the number of *encryption rounds* will also have to be increased to 12 or 14.

plaintext is *XOR*ed with the *Cipher Key* (from the *key schedule*) in the *AddRoundKey* step. During the *AddRoundKey* step for the 10 consecutive *rounds*, the resulting *block* is *XOR*ed with the *round key* generated in the *key schedule* process for that particular *round* (See Figure 5).

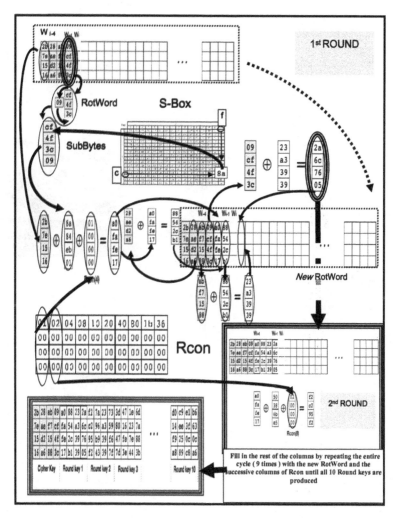

Figure 5: The Key Schedule

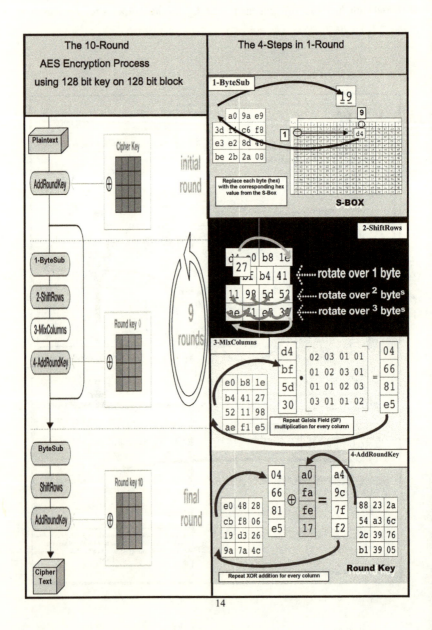

Figure 6: The Encryption Process

2.3.2 Previous Endeavours on the Cryptanalysis of Rijndael

The AES proposal states that *Rijndael* was designed to provide *"resistance against all known attacks"* (Daemen and Rijmen, 1999). Unlike most *ciphers* with *round transformation*, it is a non-*Feistel* Structure which was designed to support *high diffusion* and *non-linearity* (*ibid.*). Its design was based on the *Wide Trail Strategy* and was proven to be resistant to common *block cipher* attacks like *linear cryptanalysis*[8], *differential cryptanalysis*[9] and *truncated differentials*[10] (*ibid.*). The only *non-linear* part of the AES structure, the *substitution box (S-box)* was also designed to resist algebraic manipulations like *interpolation* attacks (*ibid.*).

Although *Rijndael* is an algebraic algorithm with a simple mathematical structure, it does not necessarily mean that it would be easy to *break* it. Up till now, there are only two main directions explored in the cryptanalytic efforts on *Rijndael*: the *algebraic attacks* on the *S-box* and the *"Square Attack"* on the *key schedule*. Figure 7 (below) and Table 1 (see Appendix) show a summary of *cryptanalytic* efforts conducted on *Rijndael* so far.

---

[8] *Linear Cryptanalysis* works by finding a high probability of predictable relationships between *input bits* and *output bits*. For example: If a *stream* of bits is *input* into the *S-box*, bit 1 of the *input* would be equal to *bit* 2 plus *bit* 4 of the *output stream;* with a certain probability (Anderson,2001). These are known as *linear trails*. *Linear Cryptanalysis* attacks are only possible for 128-*bit blocks* if the sum of predictable *input-output correlations* is significantly larger than 2^{64}. Generally, this characteristic has to apply to all except a few (about 2 or 3) *rounds*. For *Rijndael*, the designers have proven that *"there are no 4-round linear trails with a correlation above 2^{-75} and no 8-round trails with a correlation above 2^{-150}"* in Section 8.2.4 of the *Rijndael* proposal (Daemen and Rijmen, 1999). On the other hand, Fuller and Millan have also demonstrated *affine linear redundancy* trails in the AES *S-box* based on *finite field inversion* (Fuller and Millan, 2002). They have managed to map the *output* functions of the AES *S-box* to each other using *affine transformations*. (Fuller and Millan, 2002) describes in more detail how this novel method exploits the local structure of *Boolean functions* and their equivalent *classes*.

[9] *"Differential Cryptanalysis is a technique in which chosen plaintexts with particular XOR difference patterns are encrypted. The difference patterns of the resulting ciphertext provide information that can be used to determine the encryption key"* (Stallings, 2003:653). According to Daemen and Rijmen, *Rijndael* is resistant to *differential cryptanalysis* for all *block lengths* because there are no *differential trails* with a predicted *prop ratio* higher than 2^{n-1} (where n = *block length*) (Daemen and Rijmen, 1999). Hence, *differential cryptanalysis* can only work for *Rijndael* (128-bit block) if the *prop ratio* is above 2^{-127}. However, it has been proven that *"there are no 4-round differential trails with a predicted prop ratio above 2^{-150} and no 8-round trails with a predicted prop ratio above 2^{-300}"* for all *block lengths* of *Rijndael* (Daemen and Rijmen, 1999).

[10] *Truncated differentials* exploit the tendency of some *differential trails* to form *clusters* of patterns especially if the number of *differential trails* is very large for certain sets of *input* and *output differences* (Daemen and Rijmen, 1999). Please refer to (Knudsen, 1995) for a more detailed description of how this works. Although the structure of *Rijndael* is particularly susceptible to this type of attack, Daemen and Rijmen have discovered that *exhaustive key search* is still faster than this attack for 6 *rounds* of *Rijndael* and above (Daemen and Rijmen, 1999). Thus, this method of attack is inefficient because the minimum number of *rounds* specified in the standard for *Rijndael* is 10 (for 128-bit key). However, this method could be expanded or combined with other methods to achieve better results in future.

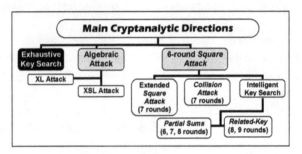

Figure 7: The Main Direction of Attacks Pursued in the Cryptanalysis of
Rijndael

One area which has created much controversy among many cryptographers is the *XSL algebraic attack* (and extension of the *XL* algorithm based on solving the root of a system of *multivariate quadratic polynomial equations[11]*) proposed by Courtois and Pierprzy (Courtois and Pierprzy, 2002). This complex mathematical solution has met with some arguments questioning its feasibility from other *cryptanalysts* like Moh and Coppersmith (Courtois, 2004; Moh 2002).

There appears to be an ongoing intellectual debate which has yet to be resolved[12] (Courtois, 2002; Moh, 2002; Courtois, 2004; Murphy and Robshaw, August 7, 2000; Daemen and Rijmen, August 11, 2000; Murphy and Robshaw, August 17, 2000). Among the papers surveyed, there are no known successful implementations to prove or disprove that the mathematical theories put forth can effectively break the full *Rijndael* as yet (Courtois, 2004; Schneier, 2002; Babbage, 2002; Danielyan, 2000; Daemen and Rijmen, 2000). This is due to the nature and complexity of the attacks,

---

[11] *Multivariate quadratic polynomial equations* are a set of *polynomial equations* with multiple variables in one *equation*. Each *term* in a *polynomial* consists of one or more (*algebra*) variables. Each variable can be expressed with an *algebraic degree* up to the *power* of 2 with a *coefficient* (a *quadratic polynomial equation*). The *coefficients* can be 0. Therefore, a *multivariate quadratic polynomial equation* consists of a *quadratic polynomial* of *multi variable terms* in one equation *i.e.* $a^2 + b^2 + c^2 + ab^2 + a^2b + cb^2 + a^2c + bc^2 + abc + ac + 1 = 0$.
Rijndael has 8000 such *equations* and 1600 *variables*.

[12] See footnote [11]. For more information, follow the chronology of papers published from the year 1999 to 2004 in Asiacrypt, Eurocrypt and Crypto Conferences. Some of these papers (online - unpublished version) can be found listed in the References section.

the design structure of *Rijndael* and the lack of computational resources powerful enough to test the proposed solutions (which are based on complex algebraic functions). Still if proven, it is still almost as slow as an *exhaustive key search* with a time *complexity* of 2^{100} (Courtois and Pierprzy, 2002).

On the other hand, the other main trend of cryptanalytic attacks on AES is based on the *"Square Attack"* [13], which is considered the best known approach to attacking *Rijndael* so far. The *Square Attack* and its subsequent existing variants (the *Collision Attack*, the *Partial Sums* Attack and the *Related-Key* Attack) are unable to break a full version of *Rijndael*. It is only successful in reducing the *complexity* for about 60 – 70% of the number of *rounds* required for a complete *Rijndael* algorithm (Ferguson *et al.*, 2000; Lucks, 2000; Gilbert and Minier, 2000; Daemen and Rijmen, 1999; Daemen and Rijmen, 1997).

The designers of *Rijndael* have foreseen the possibility of an attack on a few rounds of *Rijndael* using the *Square Attack* and set a very high minimum limit for the number of encryption *rounds* required for each *key length* to safeguard the security of the *algorithm* (Daemen and Rijmen, 1999). The best results obtained so far are for 7 out of 10 *rounds* for 128-bit *keys*, 8 out of 12 *rounds* for 192-bit *keys* and 9 out of 14 *rounds* for 256-bit *keys* (Ferguson *et al.*, 2000). This mysterious factor (which limits the number of *rounds* applicable to the attacks – about 60-70%) is holding the security of *Rijndael* at the moment.

So far, all the cryptanalytic attacks surveyed in Table 1 (see Appendix) are impractical and insufficient to reduce the *complexity* of an attack on a full version of *Rijndael*. Most of the attacks focus on the *key* or the *key schedule* (with the exception of the XL and XSL attacks which focus on the *S-box*[14]). Although the designers of *Rijndael* have made sure that an *exhaustive key search* on *Rijndael* would be impractical (if not nearly impossible) by setting a high minimum *key length*[15], the results from the variants of *Square attacks* show that the complexity is significantly decreased (2^{44} as compared to 2^{72} for a *6-round* attack on all key lengths) if combined with an *intelligent key search attack*.

---

[13] The *Square Attack* is a method used to attack 4 rounds of the block cipher *Square*. It is described in (Daemen and Rijmen, 1997). *Rijndael* is an extended version of the *Square* block cipher. The modified *6-round Square Attack* (which is based on an efficient distinguisher between 3 *Rijndael inner rounds* and a random permutation in the 4th *inner round*) on *Rijndael* (and subsequent variants) exploits the *byte*-oriented structure of *Rijndael* (Daemen and Rijmen, 1999).
[14] Their reasoning is that the *S-box* is the only *non-linear* component in AES. If the *S-box* is weakened, the rest of the components would be easy to break due to *linearity*.

[15] The minimum key length (128-bits) is more than double the minimum key length of DES (which is 56-bits).

2.4   Optimisation Heuristic Attacks

Some intelligent *cryptanalytic brute-force attacks* have been conducted on *cipher keys* using artificial intelligent methods like *simulated annealing, genetic algorithm* and *tabu search* (Kolodziejczyk, 1997; Spillman, 1993; Clark and Dawson, 1998; Lebedko and Topehy, 1998; Dimovski and Gligoroski, March 2003; Dimovski and Gligoroski, October 2003; Gründlingh and Van Vuuren). So far, these search algorithms have only been attempted on classical ciphers like *substitution ciphers* (Dimovski and Gligoroski, March 2003; Clark and Dawson, 1998; Gründlingh and Van Vuuren) and *transposition ciphers* (Dimovski and Gligoroski, October 2003; Gründlingh and Van Vuuren) as separate entities.

Nevertheless, there has yet to be an attempt to apply these algorithms to a *product cipher*. A *modern cipher* (like AES) is a *product cipher* (which is a combination of both the *substitution* and *transposition cipher*). Therefore, the results would be different (and at present unpredictable) because of the different *dispersions* caused by the combination of *diffusion* and *confusion* factors involved. However, based on the statistics observed (Kolodziejczyk, 1997; Spillman, 1993; Clark and Dawson, 1998; Lebedko and Topehy, 1998; Dimovski and Gligoroski, March 2003; Dimovski and Gligoroski, October 2003; Gründlingh and Van Vuuren), there is a good chance that there would be a general improvement in terms of search complexity as compared to an *exhaustive-key search* if these algorithms were applied in an *intelligent key-search*.

According to Clark and Dawson (who did a comparison of the three algorithms on *simple substitution ciphers*), *genetic algorithm* and *tabu search* out-performed *simulated annealing* with positive results (Clark and Dawson, 1998). The attack strategy used on the *simple substitution cipher* was based on replacing alphabet symbols from the *plaintext* message with alphabet symbols from the *known ciphertext* (*ibid*). This method was found to be weak because the *distribution* of *character frequency*[16] remained the same (*ibid*). Unlike most attacks on *substitution ciphers*, this strategy does not depend on the matching of *character frequency*

---

[16] Section 2.4.3 discusses this in greater detail.

18

statistics of a known language against the *ciphertext* (Clark and Dawson, 1998) or *plaintext* (See section 2.4.3 for more details). This implies that it would be difficult to accurately identify positive *semantic* results in the search for the *optimum solution*.

The results of this study showed that *"for a message of 1000 characters it is possible to recover 26 out of 27 key elements on the average"* (Clark and Dawson, 1998). This means that only about 2.6% to 2.7 % of the *original plaintext* message can be recovered using this method. Although the search may not produce very accurate results easily, this is considered a positive result due to the *confusion* effect caused by the nature of the *substitution ciphers*. Unlike the *transposition cipher*, the nature of the *substitution cipher* does not allow anything short of the exact same *key* used for *encryption* to completely *decrypt* the message correctly. *"Note that in practice it is impossible to find a simple substitution cipher key which differs in exactly one place from the correct key. However, it is not necessary to recover every element of the key in order to obtain a message that is readable"* (Clark and Dawson, 1998).

The results presented in (Dimovski and Gligoroski, October 2003) also show that *genetic algorithm* and *tabu search* perform better than *simulated annealing* against *transposition ciphers* (although the authors claim that *simulated annealing* is more powerful). Note that these two methods are opposites: the *genetic algorithm* introduces diversity into the *solution pool* whereas the *tabu search* prevents the same *solution* from being re-evaluated too soon.

2.4.1   Tabu Search (Glover et. al., 1993)

The *Tabu Search* algorithm maintains several *tabu lists* to represents taboo moves in *short-term* and *long-term memory*. This algorithm is usually problem-specific. An initial *solution* is generated and given a *fitness value* based on preset *criteria*. If it is not an *optimal solution*, it is replaced with a better *solution* (better *fitness value*) at the consecutive iteration (within the limitations imposed by the *tabu lists*). *Long-term tabu lists* store *frequency* values while *short-term tabu lists* store *recency* values. *Aspiration criteria* allow *taboo moves* to be executed if the overall *solution* is an improvement.

2.4.2   Genetic Algorithm (Holland, 1975)

Genetic Algorithms were first introduced by Holland to solve problems based on the *evolutionary* process of *gene reproduction* (Holland, 1975). Figure 8 (below) shows a general overview of the *algorithm* which is adapted from its biological counterpart.

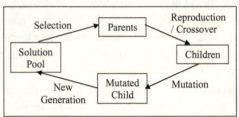

Figure 8: The Evolutionary Process.

The *genetic algorithm* begins with a pool of pre-computed *solutions* (*gene pool*). Two *solutions* (*parent chromosomes*[17]) with the best *fitness*[18] are selected from the *pool* to go through the *reproduction* process (also known as "*Crossover*"), where specific *alleles*[19] in both *parents* are swapped randomly to produce two new *children* with a combination of *genes* from both *parents*. Each *child* (*solution*) is then evaluated to determine its *fitness* value. The *fittest child* (*individual*) is selected for the next phase known as *mutation*. During the *mutation* phase, specific locations (*loci*) in the chosen *individual* (*solution*) are replaced with randomly chosen values to produce an *individual* with a better *fitness* value. The new *individual* is returned to the *solution pool* and the cycle repeats itself for the successive *generations*.

2.4.3   Letter Frequency Counts in Natural Language as a Heuristic Factor for Key Generation

The structure of an English language word consists of *unigrams* (single letter characters), *bigrams* (character pairs) and *trigrams* (character triplets). Studies have been done to determine the probability of occurrence for characters in the English language (Crypto'04, 2004). Table 2, Table 3 (see below) and Table 4 (see

---

[17] Each chromosome is usually an array of fixed length containing binary or data values predetermined by some initial criteria. Each *loci* (location in the array) contains a *gene* value.

[18] Calculation of fitness depends on the nature of the problem. The algorithm is problem-specific.

[19] Alleles are pairs of genes at the same location in each parent chromosome.

Appendix) reveal the general order of frequency for the occurrence of each character (*unigram*) and common *bigrams* and *trigrams*.

Table 2: Most Common Unigrams, Bigrams and Trigrams in the English Language Source: Crypto'04

Table 3: Simple letter frequencies, scaled to occurrences per 10 000 characters (3,117,957 characters). Source: modified from (Gründlingh and Van Vuuren)

Letter	Frequency	Digrams in decreasing order	Trigrams
E	.127	TH	THE
T	.091	HE	ING
A	.082	IN	AND
O	.075	ER	HER
I	.070	AN	ERE
N	.067	RE	ENT
S	.063	ED	THA
H	.061	ON	NTH
R	.060	ES	WAS
D	.043	ST	ETH
L	.040	EN	FOR
C	.028	AT	DTH
U	.028	TO	
M	.024	NT	
W	.023	HA	
F	.022	ND	
G	.020	OU	
Y	.020	EA	
P	.019	NG	
B	.015	AS	
V	.010	OR	
K	.008	TI	
J	.002	IS	
X	.001	ET	
Q	.001	IT	
Z	.001	AR	
		TE	
		SE	
		HI	
		OF	

A	820
B	154
C	167
D	445
E	1260
F	265
G	117
H	825
I	630
J	28
K	76
L	403
M	252
N	639
O	810
P	134
Q	3
R	537
S	622
T	871
U	269
V	101
W	249
X	6
Y	247
Z	10

These *frequency statistics* can be used to determine the probability of occurrence for each *unigram, bigram* and *trigram* in a potential password *key*. Generally, vowels are the most frequently used *character* in the English language. A *heuristic* function could be created to piece together some of these elements (*unigrams, bigrams* and *trigrams*) to form a word, which could ultimately be the correct password used to form the possible *key solution*.

Chapter 3 – Proposed Design Methodology / Framework
3.1 Overall Framework of the Proposed Solution

A known *plaintext* will be *encrypted* by the chosen *cipher* using a randomly chosen *key* of reduced length. The possible *key-solution* generated by the *heuristic* function will be used to *decrypt* the *known-ciphertext*. The resulting *plaintext* is compared to the original. The *fitness value* for the *solution* is obtained by *decrypting* the *known-ciphertext* and calculating the percentage of *character*-location matches in the *original plaintext* and the *decrypted ciphertext*. The *intelligent search* for the correct *key* combination will continue until a *solution* match has been found or the closest match has been found within the constraints of the test environment.

3.1.1 General Structure

For uniformity, a general structure of the proposed *methodology* was applied on the *Hill Cipher* (a *polygraphic substitution cipher*) *substitution,* the *Columnar Transposition Cipher* (a *permutation cipher*) and the *AES* (a *modern cipher / product cipher*). Section 3.2 and Section 3.3 briefly illustrate a general outline of the proposed *methodology* for the *Tabu Search Algorithm* (see Figure 9) and the *Genetic Algorithm* (see Figure 10). Each *series* of tests will consist of 3 *trial runs* of the *full test cycle* (1 *full round*) to obtain the average *search results* of that particular *test series*.

3.1.2 General Constraints

In order to observe the unique properties and to allow unbiased comparisons between the three different types of *cipher algorithms*, a uniform structure and environment was used to conduct the tests. The following criteria of the *cipher algorithms* were adjusted to prepare a suitable uniform environment for testing in the limited time frame given:

1. A uniform intelligent *known plaintext-known ciphertext key-search* attack using *Tabu Search* and *Genetic Algorithm* was conducted on all three types of *cipher algorithms* (*Hill Cipher, Columnar Transposition Cipher, AES Cipher*).

22

2. For the purpose of uniformity, the continuous *tests* were conducted on *Pentium IV 1.50 GHz Computer* with *256MB RAM* running on a *Linux C* platform.

3. Only *character*-location matches will be considered. Upper *hex* matches and lower *hex* matches will not be considered for uniformity *among cipher algorithms*. This is because the *confusion* and *diffusion* characteristic in the *cipher* algorithms causes the single *hex digit* match to be redundant and useless in terms of identifying patterns.

4. The *plaintext message* used for testing is limited to a standard of 16 *bytes* (128 *bit*).[20]

5. The *encryption* and *decryption* key will be limited to a fixed maximum 8-*byte* English dictionary word (8 *characters*)[21].

6. The *symmetric key* will only contain English syllables (*unigrams*, *bigrams* and *trigrams*) and common dictionary words. Numbers and symbols will not be considered (see Table 2 and Table 3).

7. Only ASCII *characters* will be considered. This will reduce the *complexity* of the attack to a maximum of 56^{16} *encryptions* (approximately 9.354 x 10^{27} *encryptions*) for an *exhaustive key search*. This would take a maximum of approximately 2.97 x 10^8 years provided 1 million encryptions are done every microsecond. Table 5 shows the ASCII *characters* used and their corresponding *hexadecimal* codes.

8. The *Tabu Search Algorithm* will search randomly for possible *key* solutions from a *pool* of known words in the English language. The length of these *keywords* can be from 1 *character* to a maximum of 8 *characters*.

9. For the *Tabu Search* test run, an assumption is made that the *plaintext message* is *encrypted* with a commonly known weak *password* included in the pool of passwords.

10. For the purpose of comparison, the *Tabu Search* test will be conducted on two separate *pools* on different occasions. The first pool contains 2,275 common passwords (8 *characters* or less) in *upper case*, *lower case* and *title case*. The second *pool* contains 72,504 common dictionary words (8 *characters* or less) in *lower case*.

11. The *Genetic Algorithm* will be constrained to search randomly for possible *8-character key* solutions from a *pool* of known syllables in the English language. This

---

[20] Due to the limited time frame, this number (16 *bytes*) is chosen for ease of testing, measurement and uniformity because the *AES* algorithm encrypts messages in 16-*byte* blocks. However, the *length* of the *plaintext* will have no bearing on the results as the attack is centered on the *key* and not the *plaintext message*.

[21] One ASCII character is represented by 8 bits (1 byte). See table 5 for equivalent *hex* digit representation.

23

pool consists of 27 *unigrams*, 30 *bigrams* and 12 *trigrams* (As shown in Table 2 and Table 3).

12. For the purpose of comparison and uniformity with the *Tabu Search* test, the *Genetic Algorithm* test will be conducted on two separate *pools* on different occasions even though the pool size has no bearing on the ultimate results. The first *pool* contains 320 common passwords (exactly 8 *characters*) in *upper case*, *lower case* and *title case*. The second *pool* contains 27,020 common dictionary words (exactly 8 *characters*) in *lower case*.

Table 5: American Standard Code for Information Interchange (ASCII) codes for 56-character set. Source: modified from cplusplus.com

Character Set (ASCII)	A	B	C	D	E	F	G	H	I	J	K	L	M
ASCII (Hex) Representation	41	42	43	44	45	46	47	48	49	4A	4B	4C	4D

Character Set (ASCII)	N	O	P	Q	R	S	T	U	V	W	X	Y	Z
ASCII (Hex) Representation	4E	4F	50	51	52	53	54	55	56	57	58	59	5A

Character Set (ASCII)	a	b	c	d	e	f	g	h	i	j	k	l	M
ASCII (Hex) Representation	61	62	63	64	65	66	67	68	69	6A	6B	6C	6D

Character Set (ASCII)	n	o	p	q	r	s	t	u	v	w	x	y	z
ASCII (Hex) Representation	6E	6F	70	71	72	73	74	75	76	77	78	79	7A

3.2　Proposed *Tabu Search* Algorithm Framework

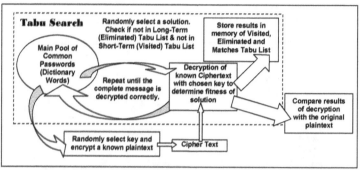

Figure 9: One Full Test Round of *Tabu Search Algorithm*

For the purpose of uniformity, consider the *encryption* and *decryption* process as a *black box*. A description of a series of test *rounds* is as follows:

1. Run steps 2-5 for the *Hill Cipher*, the *Columnar Transposition Cipher* and the *AES Cipher*.

2. Initialise 2 *Long-term memory tabu lists*: "Eliminated" and "Matches". Initialise 1 *short-term memory tabu list* "Visited" of length n/2, where n = number of *solutions* attempted from the *solution* space. Randomly select an *encryption key* from the main *solution* pool and *encrypt* the *known plaintext message*.

3. Randomly select a *solution* (*keyword*) from the main *solution* pool and evaluate the *fitness* of the *solution*. Calculate the *fitness value* for the *solution* by *decrypting* the *known-ciphertext* and calculating the percentage of *character*-location matches in the *original plaintext* with the *decrypted ciphertext*. Store the *fitness value* of the current *solution*. If the *fitness value* is zero, store the *solution* (*keyword*) in the "Eliminated" *Long-term memory tabu list*. If the *fitness value* is > 0, store the matched *character*-location value in the "Matches" List and store the *solution* (*keyword*) in the "Visited" *Short-term Tabu List*.

4. Repeat step 3 and compare the *fitness value* of the new *solution* with the old *solution*. Repeat steps 3-4 until an *exact match* has been *found*. Identify the total number of *decryptions* required to *decrypt* the *full message* correctly.

25

5. Repeat steps 2-4 twice to produce a *test series* of 3 *test rounds*. Obtain the *average* number of *search keys* required to *decrypt* the full *message* correctly.

3.3 Proposed *Genetic Algorithm* Framework

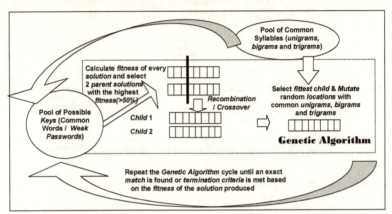

Figure 10: One Full Test Round of *Genetic Algorithm*

For the purpose of uniformity, consider the *encryption* and *decryption* process as a *black box*. A description of a series of test rounds is as follows:

1. Run steps 2-11 for the *Hill Cipher*, the *Columnar Transposition Cipher* and the *AES Cipher*.

2. Randomly select an *encryption key* from the main *solution* pool and *encrypt* the *known plaintext message*.

3. Create a new *solution pool* from the pool of common syllables (*unigrams, bigrams* and *trigrams*) and calculate the *fitness value* for all the *solutions* in the new *solution pool* by *decrypting* the *known-ciphertext* with each *solution key* by calculating the percentage of *character*-location matches in the *plaintext* and the *decrypted ciphertext*.

4. Choose two *solutions* with the *best fitness value*. Each *solution* should minimally be able to recover at least 50% of the original *plaintext message*.

5. Randomly select a "*crossover*" point and swap the contents between the two *solution key* arrays (as shown in Figure 10).

6. Evaluate the *fitness* for each new *child* (*solution key*) by *decrypting* the *known-ciphertext* with each *"child"* key and calculating the percentage of *character-location* matches in the *plaintext* and the *decrypted ciphertext*.

7. Choose the *"child"* solution with the highest *fitness value* (highest percentage of matched *character-locations*).

8. Randomly select *locations* and *mutate* the selected *locations* with arbitrarily chosen *unigrams, bigrams* and *trigrams* from the pool of common syllables.

9. Evaluate the *fitness* of the solution. If the *fitness value* is better than the *current fitness value*, update the *current fitness value* and the *best solution* variables.

10. Repeat steps 8-9 until the *fitness value* is 100% (an *optimal solution* is reached) or there is no change in *best fitness* for a predetermined number of iterations (n, where n = size of filtered solution pool).

11. Repeat steps 2-10 twice to produce a *test series* of 3 *test rounds*. Obtain the *average* number of *search keys* required to *decrypt* the full *message* correctly.

Chapter 4 – Implementation and Results
4.1 Implementation Problems

Genetic algorithm contains a *pool* of *solutions*. These *solutions* take up a lot of *memory* space. *Tabu search* contains *long-term memory tabu lists* and *short-term memory tabu lists* of *tested solutions*. This also takes up a lot of *memory* space. The total amount of time needed to get the results for intelligent *key-search* attack depends on 3 major factors: the probability of *random selection,* the weakness of the *keyword* chosen and the *strength* of the *cipher* structure against a *heuristic attack.*

Generally, the *Tabu Search test runs* were carried out smoothly without any major problems. On average, the *test runs* lasted a few hours (between 2 hours and 7 hours each). On the other hand, the *Genetic Algorithm* proved to be most efficient on *transposition cipher* (the *Columnar Transposition Cipher*) and produced results in less than an hour for each *trial run*. However, it was also observed that the *Genetic Algorithm* produced weak results for the *substitution cipher* (the *Hill Cipher*) and the *modern cipher* (the AES *product cipher*).

After many *trial runs*, it was discovered that the *processing power* of the *test environment* (*Pentium IV 1.50 GHz Computer* with *256MB RAM* running on a *Linux C* platform) was insufficient to completely recover the full *plaintext message* from these two *ciphers* (the *Hill Cipher* and the AES *product cipher*). These *trial runs* usually lasted about 8 to 12 hours each before the *platform* crashed due to insufficient *memory* to contain the ever-growing *genetic key-solution pool*. Hence, the results obtained from the *genetic algorithm attack* against the *Hill Cipher* and the AES *Cipher* were less positive than expected. Nevertheless, the attacks were successfully conducted on the *full-cycle versions* of all the *cipher algorithms* to produce measurable results.

4.2 General Findings : Results of Implementation of Proposed *Tabu Search* Algorithm Framework

Figure 11, Table 6 and Figure 12 (below) summarize the results obtained from 21 *test runs* (*7 series*) of the *Tabu Search algorithm* on the three types of *ciphers* (*AES, Hill* and *Columnar Transposition*) based on a *pool* of 2275 possible *keywords*.

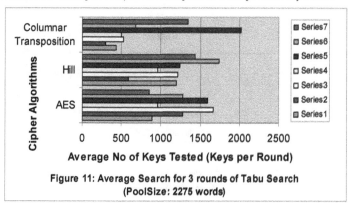

Figure 11: Average Search for 3 rounds of Tabu Search
(PoolSize: 2275 words)

Table 6: Results for 21 rounds (7 series) of Tabu Search (Pool Size: 2275 words)

	Series (3 rounds)	AES		Hill		Columnar Transposition	
		Total Search (keys)	Average (keys)	Total Search (keys)	Average (keys)	Total Search (keys)	Average (keys)
Pool Size: 2275	1	2660	886	3594	1198	1315	438
	2	3841	1280	1771	590	906	302
	3	5007	1669	3633	1211	1573	524
	4	2893	964	2889	963	1499	499
	5	4781	1593	3720	1240	6058	2019
	6	3819	1273	5226	1742	2047	682
	7	2558	852	4304	1434	4019	1339
Average (keys)		3651	3651	1217	3591	1197	2488
Percentage (%)			53		53		36

AES=Advanced Encryption Standard

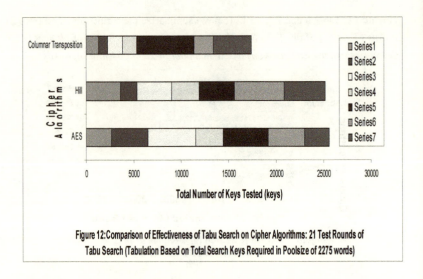

Figure 12:Comparison of Effectiveness of Tabu Search on Cipher Algorithms: 21 Test Rounds of Tabu Search (Tabulation Based on Total Search Keys Required in Poolsize of 2275 words)

Figure 13, Table 7 and Figure 14 (below) summarize the results obtained from 21 *test runs* (7 *series*) of the *Tabu Search algorithm* on the three types of *ciphers* (*AES*, *Hill* and *Columnar Transposition*) based on a *pool* of 72504 possible *keywords*.

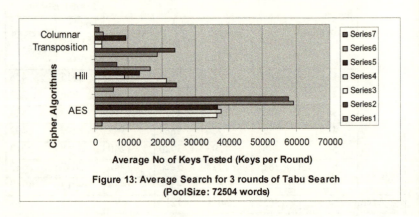

Figure 13: Average Search for 3 rounds of Tabu Search
(PoolSize: 72504 words)

Table 7: Results for 21 rounds (7 series) of Tabu Search (Pool Size: 72504 words)

	Series (3 rounds)	AES		Hill		Columnar Transposition	
		Total Search (keys)	Average (keys)	Total Search (keys)	Average (keys)	Total Search (keys)	Average (keys)
Pool Size: 72504	1	6339	2113	16592	5530	55956	18652
	2	97404	32468	72782	24260	71417	23805
	3	108919	36306	64256	21418	6445	2148
	4	112722	37574	26559	8853	6197	2065
	5	109792	36597	40249	13416	27720	9240
	6	177808	59269	4962	16547	7621	2540
	7	172919	57639	19936	6645	4106	1368
Average (keys)		112272	112272	37424	35048	13810	25637
Percentage (%)			52		19		12

AES=Advanced Encryption Standard

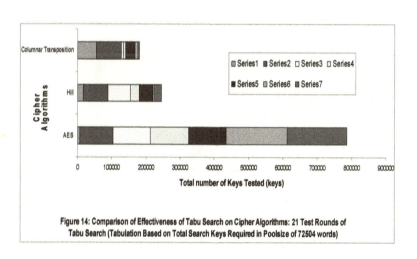

Figure 14: Comparison of Effectiveness of Tabu Search on Cipher Algorithms: 21 Test Rounds of Tabu Search (Tabulation Based on Total Search Keys Required in Poolsize of 72504 words)

4.2.1　Hill Cipher

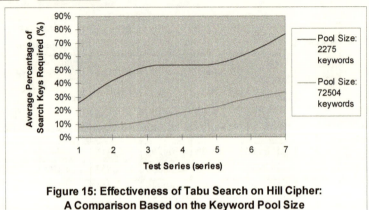

Figure 15: Effectiveness of Tabu Search on Hill Cipher: A Comparison Based on the Keyword Pool Size

4.2.2　Columnar Transposition Cipher

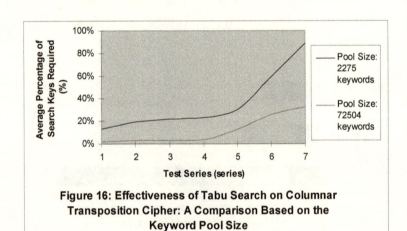

Figure 16: Effectiveness of Tabu Search on Columnar Transposition Cipher: A Comparison Based on the Keyword Pool Size

4.2.3 AES Cipher

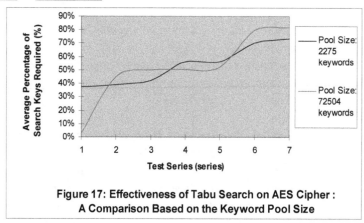

Figure 17: Effectiveness of Tabu Search on AES Cipher :
A Comparison Based on the Keyword Pool Size

4.3 General Findings : Results of Implementation of Proposed *Genetic Algorithm* Framework

For uniformity, the genetic algorithm is tested using an *encryption key* from 2 *pools* (similar to *Tabu Search*). However, the *pools* of *encryption keys* only contain *keywords* which are exactly 8 *characters* long. The sizes of the two pools are 320 *keys* and 27020 *keys* respectively. Overall, the *genetic algorithm* produced results from the *Columnar Transposition Cipher* fast and efficiently. In fact, the performance against this *cipher* was better than the *Tabu Search*.

However, the *genetic algorithm* generally did not perform well on the other two *ciphers,* namely the *Hill Cipher* and *AES*. In most of the cases, the *genetic algorithm* could not produce any significant positive result from these two *ciphers* at all. After one month of continuous test runs, it was discovered that these two *ciphers* have a consistent *pattern*: One *test run cycle* can last up till 8-12 hours before the *Pentium IV 1.50 GHz Computer with 256MB RAM* fails and *crashes* in the midst of *building* the *initial solution pool* (which contains less than desirable *key solutions*). Consequently, an important point to note is that when attempts were made to use the *genetic algorithm* on the *Hill Cipher* or the *AES Cipher*, the *process* almost never goes beyond the first step of *initializing* the *solution pool* and obtaining two *parent key solutions* with a minimum *fitness* (percentage of *plaintext* recovered) of 50% or more.

33

4.3.1　Hill Cipher

The results obtained by using the *genetic algorithm* on the *Hill Cipher* are generally more positive than the *AES cipher*. In the worst case scenario, no *parent key solution* can be found with even a 1% *fitness* using the existing *hardware technology*. Table 8 summarises the average results of the best case and average case scenario after one month of continuous *test runs*.

Table 8: Summarised Average Results for the Application of *Genetic Algorithm* on the *Hill Cipher*

	Fitness (Percentage of Plaintext Recovered)	Initial Pool Size (keys)	Generations (keys)	Estimated Average Time Span to Obtain Best Parent Solution (Hours)
Best Case	100.00%	149671	0	6.5
Average	56.25%	230600	0	4.5

4.3.2　Columnar Transposition Cipher

Table 9 (below) summarises the results of 60 *test runs* of the *genetic algorithm* on the *Columnar Transposition Cipher* obtained from Table 10 and Table 11 (see Appendix).

Table 9: Summarised Results for the Application of *Genetic Algorithm* on the *Columnar Transposition Cipher*

Exhaustive Key Search (keys)	9.67E+13
Genetic Algorithm on Columnar Transposition Cipher (keys)	2.45E+02
Percentage of search keys used over possibilities (%)	2.53E-10
Efficiency	1.00

Figure 18 summarizes the average results of conducting 10 *series* of *test runs* (total of 30 *test runs*) of the *Genetic Algorithm* on the *Columnar Transposition Cipher.*

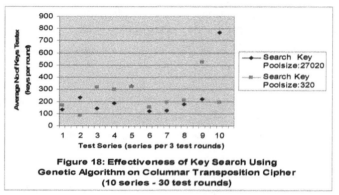

Figure 18: Effectiveness of Key Search Using Genetic Algorithm on Columnar Transposition Cipher (10 series - 30 test rounds)

Figure 19 (below) illustrates a pattern, showing the relationship between the total number of *generations* of *key solutions* required to be tested before an *optimal solution* is found vs. the *initial pool size* required to obtain 2 *parents* with a minimum fitness of 50%.

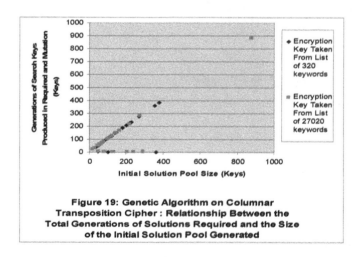

Figure 19: Genetic Algorithm on Columnar Transposition Cipher : Relationship Between the Total Generations of Solutions Required and the Size of the Initial Solution Pool Generated

4.3.3   AES Cipher

The results obtained by using the *genetic algorithm* against the *AES cipher* are the worst among the three *cipher* groups. In most cases, one *test run cycle* can last up till 8-12 hours before the *Pentium IV 1.50 GHz Computer with 256MB RAM* fails and *crashes* in the midst of *building* the *initial solution pool* (which contains *key solutions* with *fitness values* of less than 25 %). In the worst case scenario, no *parent key solution* can be found with even a 1% *fitness* using the existing *hardware technology*. Table 12 summarises the average results of the best case and average case scenario after one month of continuous *test runs*. However, an important point to note is that these results are very rare with the worse case scenario being the norm.

Table 12: Summarised Average Results for the Application of *Genetic Algorithm* on the *AES Cipher*

	Fitness (Percentage of Plaintext Recovered)	Initial Pool Size (keys)	Generations (keys)	Estimated Average Time Span to Obtain Best Parent Solution (Hours)
Best Case	25.0%	18580088	0	4.5
Average	12.5%	385592	0	2.5

4.4   Discussion of Results
4.4.1   Proposed Tabu Search Algorithm Framework

A trend was observed from the results of this research (assuming the *encryption password key* is a common word or a weak password). Regardless of the strength of the *cipher algorithm,* the performance of the *Tabu Search attack* is generally improved if the *attacker* uses a larger *pool* of known potential weak *password keys* (see Table 6, Table 7, Figure 15, Figure 16, Figure 17).

However, contrary to the characteristics of the two *classical ciphers* (the *polygraphic substitution cipher* and the *transposition cipher*) the *security* of the *AES cipher* proved to be relatively stable and did not vary too much with the change of *Tabu Search keyword pool size* (see Figure 17, Table 6 and Table 7). Although there is a very slight improvement in the performance of the *Tabu Search attack* on the *AES Cipher* with the increase of the potential *keyword solution pool size*, the changes are very minor and almost negligible.

This is surprising considering the *AES cipher* is a *product cipher* which should contain the properties of both the *substitution* and the *transposition ciphers*. It appears as if the *product cipher* has inherited more of the strengths of both types of *classical ciphers* but very little of the weaknesses. However, this proves that although the *strength* of the AES *product cipher* is affected by the *strength* of the *key* to a certain degree, the *cipher's security* is relatively stable because it does not fully depend on the *security* of the *key* alone.

4.4.1.1 *Hill Cipher*

The results obtained by using the *genetic algorithm attack* against the *Hill Cipher* are generally more positive than the *AES cipher*. This is largely because the *Hill cipher* is a *substitution cipher* without the *diffusion* properties of a *transposition cipher*, which is inherent in the *AES cipher* (*product cipher*).

The performance of the *Tabu Search attack* against the *polygraphic substitution cipher (Hill cipher)* is generally improved if the *attacker* uses a larger *pool* of known potential weak *password keys*. This is evident in the summarised results in Figure 15. Table 6 and Table 7 also show that the average number of *search keys* required is 53% (for the pool size of 2275 potential *keywords*) and 19% (for the pool size of 72504 potential *keywords*) respectively. This means that an attacker can easily retrieve the *encrypted message* if he or she has a larger bank of *passwords* to *search* from.

Furthermore, in accordance with the results obtained by (Clark and Dawson, 1998) on the *simple substitution cipher*, the *Tabu Search attack* proved to be more efficient against the *polygraphic substitution cipher (Hill cipher)* as compared to the *Genetic Algorithm* attack.

4.4.1.2 *Columnar Transposition Cipher*

Among the three types of ciphers (*polygraphic substitution cipher, transposition cipher* and *product cipher*), the *Tabu Search attack* produced the best results with *transposition cipher (the columnar transposition cipher)*. This proves that the *transposition cipher* is the weakest of all three *cipher algorithms* against the *Tabu Search attack*. Additionally, Figure 16 shows that the performance of the *Tabu Search attack* against the *transposition cipher (the columnar transposition cipher)* is generally improved if the *attacker* uses a larger *pool* of known potential weak *password keys*.

The *Tabu Search* method used here has proven to be more efficient than the method used by (Dimovski and Gligoroski, October 2003) against the *transposition cipher*. Unlike the method used by (Dimovski and Gligoroski, October 2003), the original *plaintext* message was completely recovered in a very short time (less than an hour) using this method of attack. The average percentages of search keys used were only about 36% (for the pool size of 2275 potential keywords) and 12% (for the pool size of 72504 potential keywords). Please refer to Table 6 and Table 7 for details.

4.4.1.3 AES Cipher

The attack on a *modern cipher* was conducted with a known 128-*bit* (16 characters) *plaintext block* and a known 128-bit *ciphertext block encrypted* with *128-bit cipher key* using the AES *algorithm*.

The *symmetric-key length* was fixed at 128 bits. The actual length of the *symmetric keyword* was reduced and fixed to a maximum of 8 *bytes* (64 *bits*). The remaining 8 *bytes* (128 *bits* – 64 *bits* = 64 *bits*) was buffered with blanks to reduce the complexity and cost of the searching process to 56^8.

Practical test results obtained from the *Tabu Search attack* showed that the *character* matches obtained in the list only apply to the exact complete *keyword* used for *encryption*. *Upper Hex* matches (to determine if the keyword *character* is *upper case* or *lower case*) were not found at all. Only *Lower Hex* matches were found. However, no significant relationship could be observed between the *Lower Hex* matches and the corresponding test solution's *character*-location.

Surprisingly, with the exception of conducting 1-*round encryption*, possible *keyword solutions* which were almost similar to the original *encryption key* did not produce any *character*–location matches at all. Corresponding to this, we can conclude that *character*-location matches obtained from different *solutions* (other than the actual *encryption key*) did not show any significant *semantic* or *syntactic* relationship at all[22].

Therefore, for more *1-round encryption*, only the exact *keyword* used for *encryption* could be used to obtain any significant resemblance to the original *plaintext* from the *known ciphertext*. This is due to the effect caused by the combination of the *confusion* properties in the *substitution* components and the *diffusion* properties in the *transposition* components of the AES *product cipher*. This peculiarity supports the findings of (Ferguson *et al.*, 2000; Lucks, 2000; Gilbert and Minier, 2000; Daemen and Rijmen, 1999; Daemen and Rijmen, 1997) in the '*Square Attack*'. Yet, unlike the '*Square Attack*', this method has succeeded in recovering the entire *key* and the entire *plaintext message* for the complete *10-round 'Rijndael' cycle* within the constraints of the proposed assumptions mentioned earlier.

Although the *Tabu Search attack* is rather similar to an *exhaustive key search*, it is more positive as the results in Table 6 and Table 7 show that original *plaintext* message can be completely recovered with an average of 52% - 53% of the *total search* required. This means that the performance of the *Tabu Search attack* against the *AES cipher (the product cipher)* is generally stable regardless of size of the *solution pool* containing known potential weak *password keys*.

4.4.2   Proposed Genetic Algorithm Framework

Generally, the *Genetic Algorithm attack* proved to be most efficient against the *transposition cipher*. The attack succeeded in recovering the original *plaintext message* in less than an hour for each trial run (sometimes even in less than 5 minutes). Nonetheless, it was also observed that the *Genetic Algorithm attack* produced weak results for the *substitution cipher* (the *Hill Cipher*) and the *modern cipher* (the *AES product cipher*).

This is due to the fact that the original *plaintext message* may be recovered by using an alternative *key* with similar properties as the original *encryption key* on the *transposition cipher,* but never on the *substitution cipher* or on the *product cipher*. This is because of the *confusion* property inherent in both the *substitution cipher* and *the product cipher*. Generally, the results suggest that a *parallel* implementation of the *genetic algorithm* would produce better results than the *serial* implementation done here.

---

[22] This excludes using the complete original *encryption key password to* recover the plaintext message.

4.4.2.1 Hill Cipher

The results obtained by using the *genetic algorithm* attack against the *Hill Cipher* are generally more positive than the *AES cipher*. This is largely because the *Hill cipher* is a *substitution cipher* without the *diffusion* properties of a *transposition cipher*, which is inherent in the *AES cipher* (*product cipher*). However, the worst case results of the *Genetic Algorithm* attack against the *polygraphic substitution cipher* (*Hill cipher*) are almost similar to the general results produced by the *product cipher* (*AES Cipher*).

The results of the *Genetic Algorithm* attack against the *polygraphic cipher* show agreement with those found by (Dimovski and Gligoroski, March 2003) in their study of *Polyalphabetic Substitution Ciphers* and (Clark and Dawson, 1998) in their study of *Simple Substitution Ciphers*. All the results (including this research) suggest that a *parallel* implementation of the *genetic algorithm* attack may produce better results compared to a *serial* implementation (like the method used here). Nevertheless, the results obtained here in the best case scenario (see Table 8) is significantly better than the results obtained by (Clark and Dawson, 1998), who only succeeded in recovering about 2.6% to 2.7% of the *original plaintext* message.

An interesting point to note is that the proposed *Genetic Algorithm* attack with the aid of *character-frequency statistics* may recover the full *plaintext message* within the first step of the algorithm (see Table 8). This is only possible if the *hardware platform* of the *test environment* contains enough *memory space* to contain the large *initial pool of solutions*. However, this feature is rather similar to a *brute-force attack* based on *character-frequency statistics* as the rest of the *algorithm* would not be used effectively (or even at all).

4.4.2.2 Columnar Transposition Cipher

In accordance with the results obtained by (Dimovski and Gligoroski, October 2003) and (Gründlingh and Van Vuuren), the *transposition cipher* has been proven to be easily broken by the *Genetic Algorithm attack* regardless of its complexity. Additionally, the results has also shown that the *Genetic Algorithm attack* based on the *character-frequency statistics* of a language performed much better than the *Tabu Search* against a *transposition cipher* in terms of time and computational complexity (See Table 6, Table7 and Table 9).

Figure 19 shows a distinctly unique relationship observed between the *initial genetic algorithm solution pool* and the number of *generations* (additional *solutions*) required to recover the complete *plaintext message*. The graph shows that as the size of the *initial solution pool* increases, the number of *generations of solutions* required to obtain the correct *key solution* increases at a *linear* rate. Otherwise, the number of *generations* required for the attack is almost negligible if the *fitness* of the *parent solutions* generated were near the *optimal solution*.

4.4.2.3 AES Cipher

An *exhaustive key search* for a 128-bit key (2^{128} *encryptions*) could take up to 5.4 x 10^{18} years to process if 10^6 *encryptions* are done every 1 μs. Therefore, for the purpose of this experiment, the *cipherkey* consisted of a randomly generated key of 8 *characters* (8-*byte* word) followed consecutively by blanks (8 *bytes*). Therefore, the total cost of this experiment is controlled to a maximum of 56^8 *encryptions* or 9.67 x 10^{13} *encryptions* (instead of 56^{16} *encryptions* since the keyword has been reduced to 8 *bytes*)[23]. Figure 20 (below) illustrates this.

C1	C5	C9	C13
C2	C6	C10	C14
C3	C7	C11	C15
C4	C8	C12	C16

C1	C5	C9	C13
C2	C6	C10	C14
C3	C7	C11	C15
C4	C8	C12	C16

16-byte (16 characters)
plaintext

16-byte key with 8-byte
(8 characters) keyword and
8-byte blanks (highlighted)

Figure 20: Character location in the 128-bit *plaintext* and 128-bit *cipherkey*.

As observed from the AES algorithm (shown in Figure 5 and Figure 6), the 16-byte (128 *bit*) *plaintext* is *encrypted byte-by-byte* or rather, *character-by-character* (since ASCII supports 1-*byte characters*). Each *character* is arranged from top to bottom (row-by-row), and from left to right (column-by-column). The *round-keys* are generated from the *cipher key* in 4-*byte* chunks (columns) *i.e.* the first 4 *characters* of

---

[23] There are only 56 possible alphabet characters considered for this research (A...Z).

the *cipherkey* generates the first 4-*bytes* of the *round key,* the next 4 *characters* of the *cipherkey* generates the next 4-*bytes* of the *round key* and so on. In the *AddRoundKey* step, each column of the *round key* encrypts the corresponding column of the *state* (*plaintext*). This means that each 4-*byte* chunk of the *round key encrypts* 4 *characters* of the *state, byte-for-byte.*

Therefore, an assumption was made that each *character* in a 128-*bit cipher key* encrypts the *character* located in the same corresponding *byte* location in the 128-*bit block plaintext i.e.* the 1st *character* in the *key encrypts* the 1st *character* in the *plaintext*, the 2nd *character* in the *key encrypts* the 2nd *character* in the *plaintext* and so on.

An additional theoretical observation was that the *SubByte, MixColumns* and *AddRoundKey* steps do not affect the location of each *byte* in the *plaintext* as they mainly exhibit characteristics of a *substitution cipher*. Only the *ShiftRow* step exhibits characteristics of a *transposition cipher*. For 1-*round encryption*, it was further assumed that the 4-steps do not affect the location of the 1st, 5th, 9th and 13th *character* in the *plaintext*. Hence based on the earlier assumption, if the *characters* in the 1st, 5th, 9th and 13th location of the *key* were identified[24] in the *parent key solution* (1st step of the *genetic algorithm*), we could narrow down our search to 56^6 possible character combinations for the 8-*byte keyword* for the *crossover* and *mutation* step (8 *bytes* are blanks – this eliminates 56^8 *character* combinations for the *16-byte key*).

However, further examination based on practical test results obtained from the *Tabu Search attack* showed that the *character* matches obtained in the list only apply to the exact complete *keyword*. This discovery disproves the earlier assumptions made based on the assumption that a *keyword* with a similar *character* in the same *location* would produce a similar result in the same *location*.

The *test run* results show that the assumptions only apply if the *Rijndael algorithm* was reduced to only 1-*round*. Conversely, if the method was applied to a *Rijndael* algorithm with more than 1 *round* (2-*rounds* up to 10-*rounds*), the assumptions would fail to apply. The results show that only the correct *key* would produce character matches for a full cycle of '*Rijndael*'. Even other similar *keys* with only one *character* difference would not produce any *character-location* matches or even *upper hex* matches at all. Any character or *hex* digit matches obtained from other keywords were merely coincidental and did not show any similarity to the

---

[24] The 9th and 13th character of the *cipherkey* is a null value (see Figure 20).

original *encryption key.* This is due to the mysterious *dispersion* factor observed from the *"Square" Attack.*

In conjunction with that, the results shown in Table 12 suggest that it would require a *parallel* implementation of the *genetic algorithm* instead of a *serial* implementation (like the method used here) to produce reasonably positive results and hopefully recover the entire *plaintext message.*

Chapter 5 – Summary and Future Work
5.1   Summary of Results and General Observations

Overall, the *Tabu Search attack* performed better than the *genetic algorithm attack* in terms of recovering the complete original *plaintext* provided a weakly chosen *password* is used to *encrypt* the original *plaintext message*. However, the efficiency of the *Tabu Search attack* depends on the size of the *keyword pool* and the probability that the correct *encryption keyword* is a weak *password* in the pool of known *key passwords* used to recover the *plaintext*.

Conversely, the *Genetic Algorithm attack* may eventually recover the complete *plaintext* regardless of the *key* used but the cost of searching for the correct *key* is rather expensive in comparison. Although the *Genetic Algorithm attack* proved to be most efficient on *transposition cipher* (recovered the original *plaintext message* in less than an hour for each trial run), it was also observed that the *Genetic Algorithm attack* produced weak results for the *substitution cipher* and the *modern cipher* (*product cipher*).

In summary, the results have shown that the *transposition cipher* (*Columnar Transposition Cipher*) is most susceptible to the *Tabu Search* and *Genetic Algorithm* attacks on weak passwords. This is followed by the *Polygraphic Substitution Cipher* (*Hill Cipher*), which is also vulnerable to the *Tabu Search* attack as well as the *Genetic Algorithm* attack, but at a greater time cost (provided the *encryption key* is a weakly chosen password). The *product cipher* (the *AES cipher*) is the most secure among the three. Unlike the other two, the *product cipher* is rather stable in terms of its vulnerability towards the *optimisation heuristic attacks*. Nevertheless, the *product cipher* is still susceptible to weak password attacks by the average hacker or script kiddie using a basic personal computer system. This is especially obvious from the average 52% - 53% *key search* efficiency using the *Tabu Search algorithm*. In short, regardless of the strength and security of a *cryptographic cipher*, all categories of *cipher algorithms* are vulnerable to *optimisation heuristic attacks* by a basic personal computer if the *encryption key* is a weakly chosen password.

5.2   Future Work

Due to the time constraints, the scope of this research was limited to *tests runs* conducted on a *Pentium IV 1.50 GHz Computer* with *256MB RAM* running on a *Linux C* platform. Generally, the results suggest that a *parallel* implementation of the *genetic algorithm* would produce better results than the *serial* implementation done here. Therefore, this research could be further extended by running the program on a parallel cluster machine, which has a greater capacity in terms of processing power and memory space. The test programs used in this research were all written in C *code* and can easily be ported into *Message Passing Interface* (MPI), a parallel machine language. The resulting *genetic algorithm* program can thus be run in parallel on a cluster machine.

Bibliography

1. Anderson, Ross.2001. *Security Engineering – A Guide to Building Dependable Distributed Systems*. Canada: John Wiley & Sons, Inc.pp.91-92.
2. Babbage, Steve. November 11, 2002. *Rijndael and other block ciphers*. NESSIE Discussion Forum. http://www.cosic.esat.kuleuven.ac.be/nessie/forum/read. php?f=1&i=82&t=82
3. Clark, Andrew and Dawson, Ed. 1998. *Optimisation Heuristics for the Automated Cryptanalysis of Classical Ciphers*. Journal of Combinatorial Mathematics & Combinational Computing. Vol 28. pp.63-86. http://sky.fit.qut.edu.au/~clarka/papers/jcmcc1998.pdf
4. Courtois, Nicolas T. October 17, 2004. *Is AES a Secure Cipher?* http://www.nicolascourtois.net/
5. Courtois, N.T. and Pierprzy, J. Dec 2002. *Cryptanalysis of Block Ciphers with Overdefined Systems of Equations*. Asiacrypt 2002.
6. Cplusplus.com Resources Network. ASCII Code. http://www.cplusplus.com /doc/papers/ascii.html
7. Crypto'04. 2004. *Most Common Letters, Digrams, and Trigrams in the English Language*. http://academic.regis.edu/jseibert/Crypto04/Frequency.pdf
8. Daemen, Joan and Rijmen, Vincent. September 1999. *AES submission document on Rijndael, Version 2*. http://csrc.nist.gov/CryptoToolkit/aes/rijndael/ Rijndael.pdf
9. Daemen, Joan and Rijmen, Vincent. August 11, 2000. *Answer to "new observations on Rijndael"*. http://www.esat.kuleuven.ac.be/~rijmen/rijndael/answer. pdf
10. Daemen, Joan and Rijmen, Vincent. 1997. *The Block Cipher Square*. Fast Software Encryption 1997. LNCS 1267. Springer-Verlag. http://www.esat.kuleuven. ac.be/ ~cosicart/ pdf/VR-9700.pdf
11. Danielyan, Edgar. February 2001.*AES:Advanced Encryption Standard is Coming*. ; login:, the magazine of USENIX and SAGE 26(1): 62.
12. Diem, Claus. 2004. *The XL-Algorithm and a Conjecture from Commutative Algebra*. Asiacrypt 2004. LNCS 3323. pp.323. http://springerlink.metapress.com/media/1A48DDN1WP0VWH99KP6J/ Contributions/9/Q/0/L/9Q0LN6LDDETPVXXY.pdf
13. Dimovski, A. and Gligoroski, D. March 2003. *Attack On the Polyalphabetic Substitution Cipher Using Genetic Algorithm*. Technical Report, Swiss-Macedonian

scientific cooperation trought SCOPES project. http://www.pmf.ukim.edu.mk/
~danilo/ResearchPapers/Crypto/AttackPolyalphabeticSCOPES2003.pdf

14.Dimovski, A. and Gligoroski, D. October 2003. *Attacks on the Transposition Ciphers UsingOptimization Heuristics.* Proceedings of ICEST 2003. http://www.pmf.ukim.edu.mk/~danilo/ResearchPaper/Crypto/AttackTranspositionICEST2003.pdf

15.Ferguson, Niels; Kelsey, John; Lucks, Stefan; Schneier, Bruce; Stay, Mike; Wagner, David and Whiting, Doug. 2000. *Improved Cryptanalysis of Rijndael.* Springer-Verlag. http://www.macfergus.com/pub/ icrijndael.pdf

16.Filliol, Eric. 2002. A *New Statistical Testing for Symmetric Ciphers and Hash Functions.* http://eprint.iacr.org/2002/099/

17.Fuller, Joanne and Millan, William. 2002. *On Linear Redundancy in the AES S-Box.* http://eprint.iacr.org/2002/111/

18.Gilbert, H. and Minier.M. 2000. *A Collision Attack on 7 Rounds of Rijndael.* Proceeding of the Third Advanced Encryption Standard Candidate Conference. NIST. pp.230241. http://csrc.nist.gov/CryptoToolkit/aes/round2/conf3/papers/11-hgilbert.pdf

19.Glover, Fred; Taillard, Eric; and de Werra, Dominique. 1993. *A user's guide to tabu search.* Annals of Operations Research, 41. pp. 3-28.

20.Gründlingh, Werner R. and Van Vuuren, Jan H. *Using genetic Algorithms to Break a Simple Cryptographic Cipher.* http://www.apprendre-en-ligne.net/bibliotheque/ genetic.ps

21.Holland, J. 1975. *Adaptation in Natural and Artificial Systems.* Ann Arbor, Michigan: University of Michigan Press.

22.Kolodziejczyk, Joanna. 1997. *The Application of Genetic Algorithm in Cryptanalysis of Knapsack Cipher.* Proceeding of European School on Genetic Algorithms. Eurogen '97. http://ingenet.ulpgc.es/functional/eurogenxx/eurogen97/contributed/kolodziejczyk/ht/kolodziejczyk.htm

23.Knudsen, L.R. 1995. *Truncated and higher order differentials.* LNCS 1008. Springer-Verlag. pp.196-211.

24.Lebedko, O. and Topehy, A. 1998. *On Efficiency of Cryptanalysis for Knapsack Ciphers.* Poster Preoceddings of ACDM'98 PEDC. http://www.msu.edu/~topchyal/acdm98.ps

25.Lucks, Stefan. April 2000. *Attacking seven rounds of Rijndael under 192-bit and 256-bit keys.* Proceeding of the Third Advanced Encryption Standard Candidate Conference.NIST.http://th.informatik.unimannheim.de/people/lucks/papers.html

26. Moh, T. September 18, 2002. *On the Courtois-Pieprzk's Attack on Rijndael.* http://www.usdsi.com/aes.html

27. Murphy, S. and Robshaw, M. August 7, 2000. *New observations on Rijndael.* http://isg.rhbnc.ac.uk/~mrobshaw/rijndael/rijndael.pdf

28. Murphy, S. and Robshaw, M. August 17, 2000. *Further Comments on the Structure of Rijndael.* http://www.isg.rhul.ac.uk/~sean/Response.pdf

29. Murphy, S. and Robshaw, M.J.B. 2002. *Essential Algebraic Structure within the AES.* Crypto 2002. http://www.isg.rhul.ac.uk/~mrobshaw/rijndael/aes-crypto.pdf

30. National Institute of Standards and Technology, U.S. department of Commerce. November 26, 2001. *Advanced Encryption Standard(AES).* FIPS PUB 197. http://csrc.nist.gov/publications

31. NESSIE Project. February 27, 2003. *NESSIE Project Announces Final Selection Of Crypto Algorithms.* http://www.cosic.esat.kuleuven.ac.be/nessie/deliverables/press_release_feb27.pdf

32. NESSIE Consortium. February 27, 2003. *Portfolio of recommended cryptographic primitives.* http://www.cosic.esat.kuleuven.ac.be/nessie/deliverables/decision-final.pdf

33. NSA FACT SHEET. June 2003. *National Policy on the Use of the Advanced Encryption Standard (AES) to Protect National Security Systems and National Security Information.* CNSS Policy No. 15, Fact Sheet No. 1. http://www.nstissc.gov/Assets/pdf/fact sheet.pdf

34. Schneier, Bruce. 1996. *Applied Cryptography - Protocols, Algorithms, and Source Code in C.* Second Edition. Canada: John Wiley & Sons. pp.10.

35. Schneier, Bruce. *Crypto-Gram October 15, 2000.* http://www.schneier.com/crypto-gram-0010.html#7

36. Schneier, Bruce. *Crypto-Gram September 15, 2002.* http://www.counterpane.com/crypto-gram-0209.html#1

37. Schneier, Bruce. September 22, 1998. *A Self-Study Course in Block Cipher Cryptanalysis.* http://www.schneier.com/paper-self-study.pdf

38. Search Spaniel.com. *Substitution cipher Information.* http://www.searchspaniel.com/index.php/Substitution_cipher

39. Search Spaniel.com. *Transposition cipher Information.* http://www.searchspaniel.com/index.php/Transposition_cipher

40. Spillman, Richard. October 1993. *Cryptanalysis of Knapsack Ciphers using Genetic Algorithms.* Cryptologia XVII (4). pp. 367-377. http://www.plu.edu/~janssema/ga_solve.zip

41. Stallings, William. 2003. *Cryptography and Network Security Principles and Practices*. Third Edition. New Jersey: Prentice Hall. pp.29,37-40,653.

Appendix

Table 1: Summarised Results of Identified Attacks
(Cryptanalytic Directions) on AES

(Ferguson *et al.*, 2000; Lucks, 2000; Courtois and Pierprzy, 2002; Daemen and Rijmen, 1999; Daemen and Rijmen, 1997, Gilbert and Minier, 2000)

Direction	Type of Attack	No of Rounds	Key Length	Complexity (Time)	Complexity (Data/Plaintext)	Focus of Attack
Extensions of the Square Attack	Variant of Square Attack	6	(All)	2^{72}	2^{32}	Key Schedule
	Extended Square Attack	7	128 bits	2^{200}	2^{32}	
		7	192 bits	2^{184}	2^{32}	
		7	256 bits	2^{192}	2^{32}	
	Collision Attack	7	192 bits	2^{140}	2^{32}	
		7	256 bits	2^{140}	2^{32}	
	Partial Sums	6	(All)	2^{44}	$6 * 2^{32}$	
		7	192 bits	2^{155}	$19 * 2^{32}$	
		7	256 bits	2^{172}	$21 * 2^{32}$	
		7	(All)	2^{120}	$2^{128} - 2^{119}$	
		8	192 bits	2^{188}	$2^{128} - 2^{119}$	
		8	256 bits	2^{204}	$2^{128} - 2^{119}$	
	Related-Key Attack	9	256 bits	2^{224}	2^{77}	
Attacks on *Multivariate Quadratic Polynomial Equations*	XL	(All)	128 bits	2^{330}	(8000 equations & 1600 variables)	S-box
	XSL Attack	(All)	128 bits	2^{100}	(8000 equations & 1600 variables)	S-box
Typical Brute Force Attack	Brute-Force Exhaustive Key-Search	(All)	(All)	2^{n} where n = key length $(2^{128}, 2^{192}, 2^{256})$	2^{n} where n = key length (depends on choice of implementation)	Trial and error method to guess the Actual Key (Benchmark)
Linear Cryptanalysis		4				Linear Trails
		8				
Differential Cryptanalysis		4		Not Feasible		Differential Trails
		8				
Truncated Differentials		6				Clusters of Differential Trails

51

Table 4: Diphthong frequencies, scaled to occurrences per 10 000 characters (from text of length 3,117,957 characters). Source: Gründlingh and Van Vuuren

	A	B	C	D	E	F	G	H	I	J	K	L	M	N	O	P	Q	R	S	T	U	V	W	X	Y
A	6	18	24	26	9	8	13	41	39	0	15	79	36	193	1	12	0	68	61	83	11	29	11	0	34
B	12	2	0	0	57	0	0	0	6	0	0	11	0	0	15	0	0	16	2	1	21	0	0	0	10
C	27	0	4	0	29	0	0	36	8	0	8	6	0	0	32	0	0	6	0	5	6	0	0	0	1
D	56	15	7	8	44	12	8	22	42	3	2	7	11	10	45	5	0	15	31	65	5	1	20	0	13
E	105	24	41	92	36	37	18	61	46	5	12	61	55	102	40	32	1	149	135	84	5	25	47	3	43
F	24	3	2	2	18	10	5	8	26	5	1	6	6	1	56	2	0	18	5	47	5	0	2	0	11
G	22	2	1	2	16	2	1	26	12	0	1	4	2	3	34	1	0	10	11	14	3	0	3	0	5
H	135	5	3	2	373	4	2	10	105	1	1	2	4	2	72	2	0	10	9	37	9	0	30	0	10
I	15	4	24	34	23	15	18	5	0	1	5	52	33	151	16	5	1	27	92	81	0	18	8	1	0
J	4	0	0	0	11	0	0	0	0	0	0	0	0	0	7	0	0	0	0	0	6	0	0	0	0
K	4	1	0	0	27	1	0	1	19	0	0	1	1	6	3	0	0	0	1	1	0	0	1	0	1
L	35	12	4	30	58	8	3	5	35	1	3	88	5	6	32	3	0	2	18	26	2	5	5	0	17
M	52	10	1	1	59	3	1	4	20	1	0	1	7	2	27	6	0	1	8	15	5	0	6	0	20
N	37	6	16	160	54	6	72	15	23	3	4	4	6	5	56	3	0	2	35	105	4	1	10	0	14
O	14	10	7	30	6	121	6	15	12	2	11	22	48	92	19	16	0	98	27	54	139	13	35	1	12
P	13	1	0	0	25	1	0	11	7	0	0	17	1	0	12	6	0	19	3	10	5	0	1	0	1
Q	0	0	0	0	0	0	0	0	0	0	0	0	0	0	0	0	0	0	0	0	3	0	0	0	0
R	17	7	7	28	126	9	8	13	54	1	6	6	10	16	57	5	0	6	39	45	12	7	9	0	18
S	83	12	12	7	84	13	5	68	35	1	4	7	8	10	64	18	0	12	41	88	13	1	24	0	10
T	41	9	5	6	54	8	3	416	49	2	2	7	7	4	110	3	0	21	29	41	12	0	20	0	22
U	11	6	6	10	4	2	11	5	8	0	1	17	6	24	1	11	0	51	47	43	0	0	4	0	1
V	7	0	0	0	75	0	0	0	15	0	0	0	0	0	1	0	0	0	0	0	0	0	0	0	0
W	35	1	0	1	54	1	0	55	55	0	0	2	1	9	21	0	0	3	4	6	0	0	2	0	1
X	1	0	1	0	1	0	0	0	0	0	0	0	0	0	0	0	0	0	0	1	0	0	0	0	0
Y	35	6	4	5	12	6	3	8	10	0	1	4	6	3	85	6	0	3	21	17	1	0	9	0	3
Z	2	0	0	0	3	0	0	0	2	0	0	0	0	0	0	0	0	1	0	0	0	0	0	0	0

Table 10: Results of 30 Test Rounds of Genetic Algorithm on Columnar Transposition Cipher (Encryption Key Taken from Pool of 320 words)

	Initial Pool Size (keys)	Generations (keys)	Total (keys)	Average (keys)
	80	82		
	100	102		
1	70	72	506	169
	40	44		
	34	35		
2	52	52	257	86
	74	78		
	44	48		
3	356	359	959	320
	270	275		
	64	66		
4	110	114	899	300
	148	150		
	100	105		
5	228	232	963	321
	40	43		
	46	47		
6	142	147	465	155
	48	2		
	58	62		
7	202	207	579	193
	102	106		
	122	125		
8	86	93	634	211
	380	383		
	222	227		
9	182	188	1582	527
	362	1		
	52	56		
10	104	1	576	192
Average	134	123	742	247

Table 11: Results of 30 Test Rounds of Genetic Algorithm on Columnar Transposition Cipher (Encryption Key Taken from Pool of 27020 words)

	Initial Pool Size (keys)	Generations (keys)	Total (keys)	Average (keys)
	56	62		
	132	5		
1	72	77	404	135
	218	220		
	46	53		
2	78	84	699	233
	60	65		
	78	5		
3	106	107	421	140
	206	5		
	46	50		
4	120	123	550	183
	126	5		
	290	4		
5	274	281	980	327
	240	5		
	26	31		
6	48	7	357	119
	290	7		
	18	22		
7	18	23	378	126
	86	2		
	70	71		
8	144	151	524	175
	122	126		
	50	57		
9	148	153	656	219
	164	166		
	878	885		
10	100	104	2297	766
Average	144	99	727	242

www.ingramcontent.com/pod-product-compliance
Lightning Source LLC
LaVergne TN
LVHW042349060326
832902LV00006B/493